Adam's Astronomy

Adam's Astronomy

The Original Zodiac

JANE S. POOLE

RESOURCE *Publications* · Eugene, Oregon

ADAM'S ASTRONOMY
The Original Zodiac

ISBN 13: 978-1-55635-528-8

Manufactured in the U.S.A.

Contents

Preface

THIS BOOK makes a wide sweep, embracing the story of the world from eternity to eternity. That story comprises conflict, subplots, crises, climax, and a happily-ever-after ending—all in the mind of God when he created the world.

The entrance of evil into human history did not catch God by surprise. He knew we'd mess up and he planned a solution. He had this plan announced by prophets, written in the Bible, and emblazoned across the sky. *Adam's Astronomy* focuses on the plan shown in the sky.

Long before Moses penned Genesis, someone named the stars and invented the constellations. He—or they—did it to foretell the good news of a God-man who would make things right between us and the Creator. But the constellations were pirated to promote a false religion, and their true meaning vanished for millennia.

Adam's Astronomy tells the story of those who revolted against God and those who faithfully withstood them. It describes the original constellations, introduces the one who recovered their message, and explains how she did it. The last chapter contains my own happy discovery that traits of many astronomical objects illustrate the meanings of their constellations.

While some things in this book depend on tradition, mythology and archeology, none contradicts the record of Scripture. I hope readers who don't know the Creator will see that that is possible, and those who do know him will find their faith more robust.

I'm grateful to those who read early messy versions of the manuscript and encouraged me to persevere. Particular thanks go to my husband, Andy, for help with focus and transitions; to my brother, Jim Sapp, for correcting my astronomy and challenging my assumptions; and to the Cedar Creek Writers for cheering me on.

Abbreviations

Books of the Bible—Old Testament

1 Chr	1 Chronicles
Dan	Daniel
Deut	Deuteronomy
Exod	Exodus
Ezek	Ezekiel
Gen	Genesis
Hos	Hosea
Isa	Isaiah
Jer	Jeremiah
Josh	Joshua
Judg	Judges
1 Kgs	1 Kings
Lev	Leviticus
Mal	Malachi
Num	Numbers
Prov	Proverbs
Ps	Psalms
1 Sam	1 Samuel
2 Sam	2 Samuel
Zech	Zechariah

Books of the Bible—New Testament

Col	Colossians
1 Cor	1 Corinthians
2 Cor	2 Corinthians
Eph	Ephesians
Heb	Hebrews
Jas	James

Matt	Matthew
1 Pet	1 Peter
Phil	Philippians
Rev	The Revelation
Rom	Romans

1

Primordial Astronomy

W E MIGHT imagine that the images spread over ancient sky maps always portrayed gods and goddesses. After all, they are thousands of years old. But in the beginning, people recognized only one God, the Creator of all things, and those images originally had to do with him. The Bible says the heavens reveal something about God, so let's find out what they have to tell us.

Good Start Goes Bad

God created Adam from the soil, the first human being, and then Eve from Adam's DNA. God planted a garden where he and they enjoyed each other's company.

God gave Adam and Eve everything they needed—including a moral test. One tree out of all the trees in the garden was denied them: the tree of the knowledge of good and evil. If they ate of it, God warned, they would die. *WORD - HOST = BODY of · · / learn from others.*

All was good until the serpent spoke to Eve. Was she sure God had her best interest at heart? Eating the fruit would not make her die—it would make her wise like God. Eve took the fruit, ate, gave some to Adam, and he ate. That act changed everything. In fear and shame they hid from God. They had cut themselves off from their source of life. Death entered the world.

In justice and love, God cursed the serpent and promised that some day a Deliverer would restore the broken relationship. This Deliverer would be born of a woman, that is, without human father. He would crush the serpent's head and his own heel be bruised.[1] In other words, he would overcome evil by paying the death penalty. Until that time, Adam and Eve and

---

1. "In the Bible the image [of bruising] is stark and powerful, with connotations of serious and repeated injury that is virtually a death blow." Leland Ryken et al., *Dictionary of Biblical Imagery*, 127.

their offspring must cover their guilt with the blood of a lamb. The lamb sacrifice not only hid their sin, it also pictured the coming Deliverer.

One of Adam's sons, Cain, offered God garden produce instead of a lamb. Then, angered by God's rejection, he killed his brother, Abel, who had brought the required lamb. Animosity toward the faithful is natural to those who reject God's way.[2]

Message Needed

Adam, his son Seth, and Seth's great, great, great, grandson Enoch knew God, but by Enoch's time, most of the tens of thousands of people on earth had rejected the way of the lamb.

Adam, Seth and Enoch wanted to alert people to the truth, but how could they communicate it to everyone? If they wrote a book, people might not read it.[3] If they set up a monument, people might move away. They needed a permanent reminder visible to all.

But think a moment. What did they see night after night that never changed, that naturally called to mind God's eternal character? Why not use the stars to teach God's truth!

First Astronomy

Adam and Seth lived more than nine hundred years—plenty of time to study the sky. Adam was six hundred when Enoch was born. These early astronomers knew the ways of the heavenly bodies:

- The sun measured each day by its journey across the sky;

- The moon measured each month as it waxed and waned;[4]

- The stars measured the year. While some stars seemed to rotate around one area of the sky and remained visible year round, others appeared to travel along the sun's path.[5] They rose in the east, moved across the sky, and passed out of sight in the west. After twelve months the first stars reappeared. Year after year, those stars in their unchanging patterns followed that path.

2. 1 John 3:11–13; John 15:18–21.

3. Contrary to the cave man idea, there is good evidence that from the beginning people could read and write. Henry Morris, *The Long War Against God*, 42.

4. Our calendar has been adjusted and is no longer based on the phases of the moon.

5. The sun's apparent path is called the *ecliptic*. During the year it moves from slightly north to slightly south of earth's equator projected into space, and back again.

God provided the lights in the sky for light, warmth and orientation in time. Thus they evidenced both God's power and his kindness. But to get the specific message of God's plan for our sin problem, more was needed. And so, the astronomer-prophets covered the sky with pictures of the cursed serpent and the coming Deliverer.

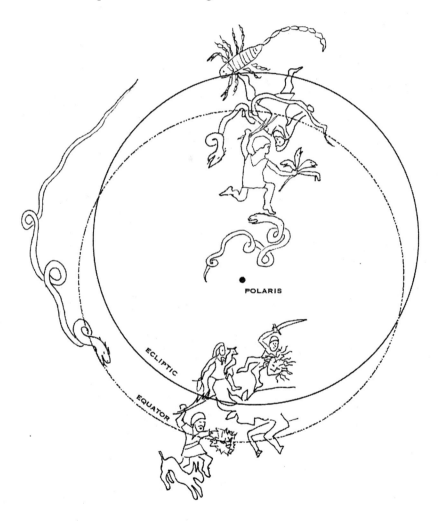

This planisphere (sky map) shows a few of the images. The serpent winds its way among the stars near the center of the sky, the foot of a kneeling human figure over its head. Above that human figure is another, who struggles with a serpent while his foot crushes a scorpion. A straight line from the scorpion through the serpent leads to a great bull and two other human figures. The foot of one is pierced by the bull's horn; the foot of the other rests on the bull's neck. Below them, one more figure threatens an unknown beast. Three of these human figures hold a severed head of a monster.

If we imagine ourselves among the first humans on earth—remembering that TV lies far in the future—part of our evening entertainment is to watch the sun set and the stars appear on the big screen above. Once in a while Great-grandfather Seth comes to visit. When all is quiet and the tiny children sleep, the older children join the grown-ups to hear Great-grandfather talk about life. He points to the starry serpent and tells about Adam and Eve's failure in the garden—how shame, sorrow and death resulted. He describes the Deliverer's foot above the serpent's head, and promises freedom some day from the serpent's power.

Designing the Zodiac

The astronomers divided the stars on the sun's path into twelve groups and gave each a picture. The twelve pictures were called *signs* because they *signified* something. God created the sun, moon and stars to have meaning as well as to mark time and provide light.[6] These twelve signs are known as the zodiac.[7]

Each sign showed some aspect of God's plan. But how did Adam, Seth and Enoch know what God's plan was? God talked with them. Only a little of what God said to Adam is recorded in the Bible, but we can imagine what they would have asked: Why did God create the world? What was he going to do about evil? When? And how?

The Bible gives good clues that God answered those questions, and also that the star signs portrayed the answers.

Clue 1: The Apostle Peter (about 64 AD) wrote

> Concerning this salvation, the prophets, who spoke of the grace that was to come to you, searched intently and with the greatest care, trying to find out the time and circumstances to which the Spirit of Christ in them was pointing when he predicted the suf-

6. Gen 1:14 AV.

7. Another name for them is Mazzaroth, Job 38:32 AV.

ferings of Christ[8] and the glories that would follow. It was revealed to them that they were not serving themselves but you.[9]

Peter pointed out that the prophets[10] tried hard to find out
1. when the promised one would come, and
2. the circumstances around his coming.

God's spirit within them predicted two stages:
1. Messiah would suffer, and
2. glories would follow.

Finally, he says God showed them that it wouldn't happen in their lifetimes but some distance in the future. That Messiah would come in the distant future made it all the more important to have a permanent reminder.

Clue 2: The Apostle Jude wrote against evil religious leaders, calling them "wandering stars for whom blackest darkness has been reserved forever," and stated that Enoch prophesied about these men.[11] Grouping *Enoch*, *prophecy* and *wandering stars* suggests that Jude knew that Enoch used the stars to illustrate his prophecies.

Clue 3: The names of Adam's descendants.[12]

The interesting thing about names is that they mean something. It appears that the names Adam and Seth chose for their direct line of descendants held the same message as the star signs:

Adam = man
Seth = appointed
Enos = mortal, incurable
Cainan = building a nest
Mahalaleel = praise of God
Jared = descend
Enoch = disciplined, dedicated
Methuselah = man of the dart or branch, shoot forth
Lamech = wounded
Noah = rest

The message in the names might be written like this: Mankind is appointed to death. To make us into his own possession, the "Praise of God,"

---

8. *Christ* is Greek for *Messiah*, the Hebrew designation for the Deliverer.

9. 1 Pet 1:10–12.

10. Enoch was a prophet, Jude 14.

11. Jude 13–15.

12. Gen 5.

5

will descend, dedicated to shoot forth against the enemy, be wounded and bring salvation.

Clue 4: The Bible says God named the stars.[13] When God walked with Adam and asked him to name the animals, might not he have shared with Adam the names he himself gave the stars? Maybe star names mentioned in the Bible[14] are names God told to Adam.

Clue 5: God may have given these early astronomers the whole plan for the signs just as he gave other people exact plans:

- Noah: measurements, materials, design for the ark[15]
- Moses: measurements, designs, materials, colors for the Tabernacle, its furniture, the priests' garments, and the recipe for holy incense[16]
- Joshua: battle plan for conquering Jericho[17]
- Gideon: battle plan for defeating the Midianites[18]
- David: plans for the Temple which Solomon would build: "All this," David said, "I have in writing from the hand of the LORD upon me, and he gave me understanding in all the details of the plan."[19]

Clue 6: In his sermon at the Areopagus in Athens, which is recorded in Acts 17, the Apostle Paul quoted from the *Phainomena* written by the Greek poet Aratos.[20] This work describes forty-five constellations as they were known about 2000 BC. Why would Paul be interested in the constellations? Being surrounded by paganism, perhaps he wanted to better understand the people he ministered to. But in so doing, did he discover for himself the true message hidden in those constellations? Apparently so, judging by what he wrote in Romans 10:18 (Clue 7).

Clue 7: The Apostle Paul testified that the "good news" was heard in the message of the heavens. In Romans 10 he argues that Israel has had many opportunities to accept the good news, and quotes from Psalm 19 in

13. Isa 40:26 and Ps 147:4.
14. Job 38.
15. Gen 6:14–21.
16. Exod 25–30.
17. Josh 5:13—6:5.
18. Judg 7.
19. 1 Chr 28:19.
20. Acts 17:28.

support: "Their voice goes out into all the earth, their words to the ends of the world," a beautiful passage about the heavens declaring God's truth.

The First Zodiac

It's impossible to know for certain, but the earliest zodiac pictures appear to have been these. They agree with Bible images and themes:

1. A woman. The promise of a deliverer to be born to a virgin.
2. A circular altar. God's justice demands sin be atoned for by blood sacrifice.
3. A scorpion. The enemy of God and mankind.
4. An archer, arrow on string. One will be sent forth against the enemy.
5. A sacrificial goat. The sacrifice for our atonement.
6. An urn pouring out water. Blessing poured on the redeemed.
7. Two fish joined with a band. Multitudes of the redeemed.
8. A ram or lamb. The sacrificed one now victorious.
9. A charging bull. He comes to rule.
10. Twins. The dual nature of the Deliverer—God and man.
11. A sheep or cattle fold. The Deliverer's possession, his people safely gathered.
12. A lion. He will trample his enemies.

These twelve signs and thirty-six other ancient constellations, known as decans, make a total of forty-eight constellation pictures. This zodiac was so effective in portraying God's plan that the enemy sabotaged it.

2

Piracy and Perversion

NIMROD, GREAT grandson of Noah, set himself up as a hero among the people, a real dragon-slayer.[1] Many followed him in revolt against God's authority. It didn't seem to matter that God's authority benefitted them, or that God had actually given *them* authority through two patterns for living: the Dominion Mandate and the Patriarchal System.

The Dominion Mandate

Back in the beginning, God directed Adam and Eve to "fill the earth and subdue it. Rule over the fish of the sea and the birds of the air and over every living creature that moves on the ground."[2] This mandate expected people to

> *spread out* over the earth,
>> *study* nature and *share* its resources,
>>> and do all this *under God's authority.*

Nimrod chose to
>> operate *by his own authority*,
> *hoard* earth's resources,

and *concentrate* people in cities.

Adam started work on the mandate by tending the Garden of Eden and naming the animals.[3] His children continued the work when they married and established homes. Marriage alone didn't provide enough structure to fulfill the Dominion Mandate, however. The next level of organization was the Patriarchal System. Nimrod had a replacement for that idea, too.

---

1. Gen 10:8–9. The Bible calls Nimrod "a mighty hunter before the LORD." "Before" is in the sense of *against* or *in the face of* the LORD. Henry Morris, *The Long War Against God,* 250.

2. Gen 1:28.

3. Gen 2:15, 19, 20.

The Patriarchal System

A patriarch was the father of a line of descendants. He spoke with authority and he worked on his family's behalf. God knew everyone's need for a loving, watchful father. If a father failed, there was grandfather or great grandfather to take that role. Ultimately, God himself is the loving, watchful father. The patriarch acted as

- a priest, to bless and pray for them
- a businessman, to oversee their economic fortunes
- a spokesman, to negotiate with outsiders
- a prophet, to pronounce God's truth to them
- a judge, to settle disputes
- and a teacher, advisor, and role model.

These men were examples of godly patriarchs:

- Adam and Seth named their descendants for the prophecy of the coming Deliverer.
- Noah built an altar and sacrificed offerings for his family.[4]
- Job offered burnt offerings for his grown children after their house parties, in case they had sinned.[5]
- Abraham rescued his nephew, Lot, after he was kidnapped.[6]
- Abraham negotiated with the Hittites to buy a family burial site.[7]
- Isaac dug wells for his family.[8]
- Jacob moved his descendants to Egypt because of famine in their land.[9]
- Jacob blessed his sons and grandsons, prophesying their character and futures.[10]

---

4. Gen 8:20.
5. Job 1:4–5.
6. Gen 14.
7. Gen 23:1–20; 49:29–32.
8. Gen 26:19–22.
9. Gen 46:5–7, 26–27.
10. Gen 48–49.

Examples of *ungodly* patriarchs were

- Cain, who murdered his brother Abel and "went out from the LORD's presence."[11] His descendants accomplished remarkable things, but they may have practiced exaggerated revenge.[12]

- Ham, whose disrespect for his father brought a curse on his descendants.[13]

The patriarchal system provided safety and security. Like a shepherd caring for his sheep, a man watched over his descendants, alert against evil. Unfortunately, apart from some of Seth's descendants, few men followed through on the stand-against-evil part. It is sad when a father fails his responsibility because

Good – Good = Not Good

When the good (God) is rejected, what's left is the not good—broken homes, crime, a messed up society. The righteous descendants of Adam and Seth couldn't overcome the deluge of immorality and violence that filled the earth.[14]

A New Start

God's solution to the problem was thorough. Only eight people survived the Great Flood: Noah, his wife, his three sons, and their wives. They survived only because God told Noah what was coming and how to prepare, and Noah believed him. If we think of all the violence and suffering in the world today, we get an idea of what Noah's world was like, since Jesus foretold the same situation would appear in the end.

God's judgment provided a fresh start. Noah, Japheth, Shem, Ham and their wives stepped out of the Ark into a changed world. Nothing of their former life was left but what they brought with them.

God instructed Noah's sons to multiply and spread out over the earth. He restated the Dominion Mandate, with some differences:

1. At the beginning, humans and animals all ate plants.[15] Now God gave animals as food, and the animals began to fear humans.[16]

11. Gen 4:16.
12. Gen 4:23–24.
13. Gen 9:18–27.
14. Gen 6:5–13.
15. Gen 1:29–30.
16. Gen 9: 2–3.

2. Before, God did not allow Cain to be killed for murdering his brother.[17] Now God gave the patriarchs authority to take a life for a life.[18]

3. Once the tropical climate produced food year round. Now there would be summer and winter, seed time and harvest.[19]

The Hunter

All was not right with the new patriarchs, however. Ham, Noah's youngest son, acted indecently toward Noah which resulted in the curse upon Ham's son, Canaan. Ham's name means *hot, inflamed*. If that reflected his character, he was not a good kind of father. It's no wonder that Canaan wasn't his only son in trouble. Cush also rebelled and then Cush's son, Nimrod. What started in Ham became worse in Cush—and horrendous in Nimrod.

> *From the root of that snake*
> *will spring up a viper,*
> *its fruit will be a darting, venomous serpent.*[20]

Now that wild animals feared man, they became a threat.[21] Nimrod gathered people into cities and built fortified walls around them. While walls do protect inhabitants from wild animals, *fortifications* are for an entirely different purpose—organized warfare. Instead of following the shepherd model of leadership, Nimrod took the hunter model—domination by force.

Replacing God

Nimrod further rebelled by creating a religion to replace God. The heavenly bodies readily evoked things eternal, mysterious, spiritual and infinite. Nimrod turned the sun, moon, planets and certain stars into gods. The Babylonian Creation Epic credits the god Marduk (whom some believe to be a representation of Nimrod) with measuring the heavens and assigning

17. Gen 4:13–15.

18. Gen 9:5–6.

19. Gen 8:22.

20. Isa 14:29.

21. Even centuries later when Israel's descendants reentered Canaan this was true, Exod 23:28–29.

stations to the constellations. This suggests that Nimrod took credit for the signs and used them in his religion.

The headquarters of the new worship was to be a magnificent structure which would serve as both temple and astrological observatory. Construction of this edifice ended abruptly when God intervened by confusing human language. What a blow to Nimrod's plans when various language groups abandoned the work at Babel! But Nimrod was not a quitter. He stayed to salvage what remained and expand his power.

Kings versus Patriarchs

The kings of the earth take their stand and the rulers gather together against the LORD and against his Anointed One. "Let us break their chains," they say, "and throw off their fetters."[22]

Nimrod's kingdom began in the land of Shinar on the plain between the Tigris and Euphrates Rivers. He ruled Babylon, Erech, Akkad and Calneh, probably through puppet kings.[23] The numerous ancient cities of Mesopotamia named for Nimrod evidence his widespread influence. An observer as late as 1876 stated that "Iraqi and Iranian Arabs still speak his name with awe."[24]

Greek and Roman myths tell of the younger gods (the Olympians) overthrowing the elder gods (the Titans). Some believe these myths refer to Nimrod's revolt against the patriarchs. Nimrod, leader of the younger gods, became known as Zeus to the Greeks, Jupiter to the Romans, and Marduk to the Babylonians. The myths portray the younger gods as deceitful, immoral and violent.

Nimrod's "nature religion" allowed a lifestyle unburdened by a moral standard. Polynesian myths tell of people so pressed down by the sky that they had to crawl on all fours until a god or a hero pushed up the sky. In other words, Nimrod and his followers got the heavens—God's standard of morality enforced by the patriarchs—off people's backs.

Romans 1:18–32 tells how nature religions like Nimrod's develop:

1. People stop thanking the Creator for his blessings, v 21. This may seem a small thing, but wanting something other than God's goodness is the dragon's egg.

---

22. Ps 2:2–3.
23. Gen 10:10
24. George Smith quoted by Bill Cooper, *After the Flood*, 189.

2. They claim to have wisdom, v 22. The serpent enticed Eve with a promise of wisdom. From ancient times to now people have worshiped the serpent (or dragon) as the source of wisdom. People who receive the serpent's wisdom, however, find that its end is slavery, darkness and death.

3. They worship images—man, birds, animals, reptiles—instead of God, v 22. Certain animals are held to hold desirable powers. Perhaps entertainment and sports superstars fit here.

4. They become sexually impure, v 24.

5. They replace the truth about God for a lie, v 25. One lie is "The earth created itself."

6. They worship and serve created things, v 25. Shopping mania, perhaps?

7. They turn to homosexuality, v 26–27.

8. They engage in all forms of wickedness, from greed to murder, v 29–30. Cannibalism is sometimes part of these religions.

9. They get Attitude!—insolence, arrogance and boasting, v 30–31. Behaviors they might once have been ashamed of they now flaunt.

10. They encourage others in this behavior, v 32. How many children take their first drink because someone urged them to? How many stole something on a dare? Witchcraft lessons, certain sex education programs, gay parades, pressure to be tolerant—all encourage wrong behaviors.

What makes all this attractive is *power*. The nature religion Wicca, for example, lets the individual be in charge. Wiccans set up their own altars, invent their own rites and spells, choose their own gods (spirit guides, totems), and decide what conduct their gods require or allow. They have no judge to be accountable to, no moral standard to live up to, no punishment to fear. They can believe that death is simply part of the great cycle of life and they will be absorbed into the cosmos or come back in another life. And, they have plenty of encouragement along this path.

A private religion may satisfy a person who wants only to control his own life, but some people want to control others. Religion is a path to power. Witch doctors, gurus, rabbis, imams, popes, and televangelists sway millions.

What if a religious leader is also a political or military leader? What if his gods demand gold or blood? This was Nimrod's religion exactly: hoards of gold and bloody human sacrifices.

When the time was right, Nimrod moved north into Assyria, where he built the cities of Nineveh, Rehoboth, Ir, Calah and Resen.[25] The kings of these cities acted as priests of their chosen deity, and sometimes they demanded to be worshiped as the deity himself.

Now Assyria had been settled by Shem's son, Asshur. Either because the new religion attracted him or because of fear of annihilation by Nimrod's armies, it appears that Asshur converted to Nimrod's way of doing things. It is believed that he became King Puzur Asshur I, one of the earliest men to be deified and worshipped by his descendants.[26] If true, righteous Shem must have been deeply affected when one of his own sons fell under Nimrod's spell.

It's possible that Shem used his influence to bring Nimrod to trial in Egypt for crimes against God and humanity.[27] There the courts ruled for execution and against burial. Nimrod's body was cut into fourteen pieces, and the pieces sent to chief cities as a horrifying warning to everyone.[28]

25. Gen 10:11–12.

26. Bill Cooper, *After the Flood*, 170.

27. Alexander Hislop arrived at this conclusion by comparing Chaldean myths and ancient Egyptian law, *The Two Babylons*, 63.

28. This practice is used in two places in the Bible: by King Saul, 1 Sam 11:7; by a Levite, Judg 19:29.

3

The Wicked Queen

NIMROD'S DEATH did not end the false religion; it had already spread across the world. But several hundred years after his death, Babylon's religious influence had a resurgence through a young and beautiful[1] queen named Semiramis. She was the widow of Ninus, the king who built the Assyrian Empire and ruled it from Babylon.

Semiramis was another man's wife when Ninus took her for himself and married her. After his death (which she may have been accused of causing), the queen reigned forty-two years. She died at sixty-two, so must have been about twenty when widowed. Semiramis constructed large brickworks to stop flooding in Babylon, added Ethiopia to her dominions, and made war on India.[2] But the power of her influence was greatest in her poisonous mystery religion.

Before continuing we must understand the chronological uncertainties of this story. Anything before about 800 BC can be considered part of the "dim past," and dating is difficult for many reasons:

- Primary sources of ancient history, other than the Bible, are often contradictory.

- Kings obliterated records of their predecessors and enhanced their own accomplishments.

- Archeologists interpret artifacts according to their presuppositions about how long mankind has existed and how civilization developed.

- Vast quantities of discovered artifacts have never been analyzed or written about.

---

1. Semiramis once supposedly quelled an uprising on the strength of her beauty alone. Her subjects' admiration was memorialized by a statue of her as she appeared at the time. Alexander Hislop, *The Two Babylons*, 74.

2. James Ussher, *The Annals of the World*, 54–55.

- Carbon dating is based on an assumed original amount of Carbon 14 and an assumed steady rate of decay.

The Semiramis described above, the wife of Ninus, reigned one thousand years after Nimrod built Babylon. Some historians hold that Semiramis lived during an earlier period, that she was the wife of Nimrod, also called Ninus,[3] and that the two of them were responsible for all idolatry—Nimrod being the prototype of many pagan gods and Semiramis the prototype for all the goddesses.

If the later date for Semiramis is correct, she could not have started idolatry. (Israel's law forbade pagan practices before then.)[4] Yet she definitely had a hand in Babylonian religious influence.

Nimrod's fame and notoriety was not forgotten in that thousand years, and any ruler associated with his name would gain status—much like Saddam Hussein's effort to be the second Nebuchadnezzar. Perhaps Semiramis was able to build her power by selling the idea that Ninus was a reincarnation of Nimrod.

She may also have made Nimrod into the promised Deliverer, claiming he had died while crushing the serpent with his heel, and accusing Shem and the patriarchal system of being the serpent. This idea appears in the religions of many cultures:

- In Egypt, the god known as Horus pierced the snake's head with a spear.

- In Greece, Apollo slew the serpent Pytho. Hercules strangled serpents in his cradle. Achilles was vulnerable only in the heel.

- In India, Vishnu as Krishna slew the serpent Calyia. Krishna died, shot in the foot by an arrow.

- In Scandinavia, Thor bruised the head of the great serpent with his mace.

- In Mexico, the great spirit Teotl crushed the serpent, the evil genius.

---

3. Alexander Hislop, *The Two Babylons*, 6n‡.

4. These included cutting or tattooing the body for the dead; making images to worship; sorcery, divination, soothsaying; sacrifices to gods, particularly sacrificing children; sacred pillars; eating blood; making their daughters harlots; homosexuality, incest and bestiality. Exod 20, 22–23; Lev 18–20; Num 19–20.

She may have begun the memorial weeping for the dead god (Nimrod) and worship of relics:

- Egyptian women, along with the goddess Isis, wept for the dead Osiris. Isis searched for scattered parts of Osiris' body, and buried each on the spot.

- Greek women wept for Adonis—the huntsman lamented by Venus.

- Phoenician, Assyrian, Israelite women wept for Tammuz.[5]

- Roman women wept for Bacchus—"the bewailed one." During that worship a fawn was torn in pieces to commemorate what happened to Nimrod.

- Iceland and Scandinavia wept for Balder.

- China wept for Wat-yune. The tartars did a yearly search for the bones of Buddha.

- India wept for Krishna.

Reinventing Semiramis

If Semiramis could increase her influence by promoting the dead Nimrod, why not promote the living Semiramis? Maybe she could identify herself as the reincarnation of the original goddess from whom all fertility goddesses developed!

She gave birth to a child, and claimed that this child, Ninus (or Ninyus), was the reincarnation of Nimrod. She made out that this birth was miraculous, and she was the virgin mother of a god. Mother and child images turned up everywhere.

- Persia, Syria, and the kings of Europe and Asia worshiped a "mother of the gods."

- Rome regarded Vesta as "mother of the gods."

- Tibet and China honored "the virgin mother of god."[6]

- Druids in Britain worshiped the "virgin mother of god"

5. Ezek 8:14.

6. Alexander Hislop, *The Two Babylons*, 77.

17

Under many different names, the virgin mother developed into the "Perfection of female beauty," the "Habitation" or "Dwelling-place (of god)" and, as worshiped in Israel, "Queen of Heaven."[7]

It would be interesting to know how much control the Babylonians had over other kingdoms through their priesthood, and how much Semiramis benefitted personally. Did she ever satisfy her ambition?

Persistence of Paganism

Paganism and the mystery religions were in full force when the Deliverer came. The Roman Empire not only imported gods from the territories it ruled, it also spread the cult of emperor worship from Rome to all parts of the Empire. As the first believers in Messiah shared the good news of deliverance, people's lives changed. The Apostle Paul wrote this to the believers at the great city of Corinth:

> Neither the sexually immoral nor idolaters nor adulterers nor male prostitutes nor homosexual offenders nor thieves nor the greedy nor drunkards nor slanderers nor swindlers will inherit the kingdom of God. And that is what some of you were. But you were washed, you were sanctified, you were justified in the name of the Lord Jesus Christ and by the Spirit of our God.[8]

How wonderful to leave a life of dissipation and darkness, to be cleansed and become the special possession of the heavenly Father!

Although Christianity changes individual lives, paganism will exist right up to the end of the world. Judaism failed to eradicate it, as did Islam and Christianity. Sometimes local pagan beliefs and practices were even incorporated into those faiths. The book of The Revelation says that in the end times God will send plagues on the earth warning people to turn and accept his mercy, yet

> The rest of mankind that were not killed by these plagues still did not repent of the work of their hands; they did not stop worshiping demons, and idols of gold, silver, bronze, stone and wood—idols that cannot see or hear or walk. Nor did they repent of their murders, their magic arts, their sexual immorality or their thefts.[9]

Here are a few elements of paganism which we easily recognize:

7. Jer 44:15–19.
8. 1 Cor 6:9–11.
9. Rev 9:20–21.

1. Drugs. The rite of initiation into the mysteries included drinking beverages of which wine was one of the ingredients and very likely hallucinatory drugs as well. Goddesses were often represented holding a cup. The prophet Jeremiah made a pun on this cup when he warned that God would use Babylon as a cup to pour out punishment on nations that accepted its idolatrous religion: "Babylon was a gold cup in the LORD's hand; she made the whole earth drunk. The nations drank her wine; therefore they have now gone mad."[10]

When Cyrus conquered Babylon in 539 BC, the booty supposedly included Semiramis' cup which weighed 1200 pounds.[11] The Apostle Paul had this in mind, as well, when he warned, "You cannot drink the cup of the Lord and the cup of demons too; you cannot have a part in both the Lord's table and the table of demons."[12]

2. Horns and Crowns. Nimrod's role as a hunter inspired the wearing of horns and crowns. Horns symbolized power and points on crowns mimicked horns. Horns were prominent in paintings, sculptures, and tattoos as seen on mummies. In goddess worship the reindeer is prominent, perhaps because the female has antlers as well as the male. Who isn't familiar with the horned Viking helmets, headgear of Native American buffalo dancers, and helmets of the Samurai leaders.

3. Mutilation of the Body. Tattooing, body piercing, branding and self flagellation were forbidden to followers of God because they were connected with the worship of the dead: "Do not cut your bodies for the dead or put tattoo marks on yourselves. I am the LORD."[13] *The dead* may refer to the dead Nimrod, or it may refer to worship of or prayer to any of the dead.

4. Science apart from God. The Egyptian pyramids, Stonehenge, Nazka dessert markings, Inca structures, Mayan calendars and ancient North American medicine circles reveal accurate astronomy and amazing feats of architecture. In those religious cultures knowledge and science belonged to the elite. This knowledge was used for fearsome, bloody violence.

Good science fulfills the Dominion Mandate through research and discovery. Under God, it improves life and relieves suffering. But under a godless philosophy, and combined with political power, the helpless can be killed and their organs harvested.

10. Jer 51:7.

11. Alexander Hislop, *The Two Babylons,* 5n**.

12. 1 Cor 10:21.

13. Lev 19:28.

5. Worship of dragons and serpents, gold and jewels of which *National Geographic*'s articles on archeology provide plenty of evidence. Burial sites the world over hold or held the treasure caches of the elite. One can only imagine the hardship of the people forced to provide those riches. Today's fascination with the power of crystals seems to reflect the dragon's connection with jewels.

6. Astrology. The belief that the heavenly bodies influence human lives and events naturally followed the acceptance of these bodies as gods. Here are a few examples of myths that replaced the original constellation meanings (original meaning in parenthesis):

- Andromeda (God's people chained and afflicted by the enemy). Greece: Andromeda chained by her parents to a rock as a sacrifice to the sea monster, Cetus, to appease the sea god.

- Auriga (the Shepherd). Rome: Charioteer, son of the god Vulcan, who invented the chariot to move his crippled body.

- Cancer (the Deliverer's gathered people). Greece: the crab sent by Hera to distract Hercules while he fought the monster Hydra, and though crushed by Hercules, given a place among the stars.

- Capricornus (the sacrifice). Greece: The god Pan whose horns identify him as Nimrod, leaped into the Nile while fleeing Typhon (Shem). The part of him under water turned fish, the top remained goat.

- Centaurus (despised sin offering). Greece: The wise centaur, Cheiron, wounded and then allowed to die even though immortal, for the benefit of another.

- Coma (virgin with the child, *the desired one*). Renamed Coma Berenices, *Hair of Berenice*, for the wife of Ptolemy III of Egypt. She sacrificed her hair to Aphrodite for her husband's safe return, but the hair was stolen, and to console her the court astrologer said the gods placed it in the heavens. In both Greek and Latin *hair* is pronounced much like *coma*. Only the sound of the name remains.

- Hercules (mighty one, sinking in conflict, yet victorious). Rome: Hercules, half-mortal son of Jupiter, who performed great exploits.

- Lyra (harp, praise). Greece: Harp of Orpheus who was torn apart by the women he spurned (allusion to Nimrod's dismemberment?)

- Orion (light bearer). Babylon: Tammuz. Greece: great hunter. Egypt: soul of Osiris.

- Sagittarius (archer coming forth from God). Nimrod, the mighty hunter.

- Taurus (ruler, judge). Egypt: Apis, bull of Memphis, incarnation of Osiris (Ninus); symbol of strength and fertility.

- Virgo (a virgin will bear the deliverer). Egypt: Isis. Babylon: the fertility goddess Ishtar. Rome: Astrea, goddess of justice. Greece: Demeter, goddess of the harvest.

Certain elements in these stories—such as a great exploit by a hero, someone he would save, his supernatural birth, and his victory over the enemy in spite of apparent defeat—recall the original prophecy of the Seed of the woman who would crush the serpent's head and be wounded in the process. However, the Deliverer's glory is given to others, and humanity's need for a redeemer is missing.

The stories spread so widely, and in so many forms, it's a wonder that anyone remembered the original meanings of the star pictures.

Yet, some did.

4

A Few Good Men

THE PREPONDERANCE of paganism did not overcome all faith in God. Neither did the perverted constellations obliterate the true. No matter how bad things get, God always has a few faithful followers.

Noah and Shem

How many times did Noah and Shem tell the story of the flood? Maybe thousands. Noah lived for 350 and Shem for 500 years afterwards. The Great Flood so powerfully demonstrated God's judgment on evil and his mercy toward those who trust him that it never disappeared from the memories of the world's people groups. One wonders if Noah and Shem added the ship Argo[1] to the sky's constellations.

Life spans decreased, as God had forewarned,[2] and by the time of Abraham, 120 years was usual.

Abraham

Abraham's family was among the nearly 360,000 people living in and around the city of Ur. Citizens resided in two-story villas of thirteen or fourteen rooms filled with gorgeous art, jewelry, clothing and musical instruments. We might think life there was happy. But Ur was one of those cities where the king and his elite priests controlled everything.

The city was dominated by five fortress-like temples surrounding the king's ziggurat. Priests received the people's sacrifices and collected taxes in oil, cereals, fruit, wool, and cattle. These went into vast warehouses. Sacrifices cooked in temple kitchens, bread baked in temple ovens, goods made in temple-owned factories to be sold in temple shops added nicely to the moon god's treasury.

---

1. See Argo under Cancer in Appendix A and number 34 Argo in Chapter 7.
2. Gen 6:3.

Although a descendant of Shem, Terah, Abraham's father, was an idolater.[3] How then did Abraham learn to know God?

Perhaps like Gilgamesh, in the Mesopotamian epic, who searched out his ancestor Utnapishtim to hear the story of the flood and the secret of life, Abraham sought out Shem. Shem would have taught him how the lamb sacrifice foreshadowed the coming Deliverer. He may have shared the original star signs. A tradition holds that Abraham taught Chaldean (Babylonian) astronomy to the Egyptians.[4] If so, Abraham's encounter with Shem might account for differences between Chaldean and Egyptian astronomy.

Abraham heard and obeyed God's call to leave Ur and go to Canaan. God promised him three things:

- to make him into a great nation,
- to give his descendants the land of Canaan, and
- to bless all the peoples of the earth through him.[5] This last part meant that the Deliverer would be one of Abraham's descendants.

The land of Canaan was already occupied by descendants of Ham's son, Canaan, and evidenced the curse Noah had put on them. They worshiped fertility gods and goddesses, and practiced all those detestable things God forbade his people.

One of Nimrod's copy kings, Kedorlaomer, controlled five Canaanite kings in the Dead Sea area. After twelve years these five kings rebelled. Elam, Kedorlaomer's distant kingdom, lay east and north of the Persian Gulf. Perhaps the five kings thought Kedorlaomer wouldn't bother to come so far to squash their revolt.

They were wrong. He came, bringing three other kings with him, and they made it worth their while. In a wide swoop, the four kings took the territories of six people groups surrounding the five kings. Genesis 14 describes the campaign.

It must have been intimidating to have their neighbors wiped out, yet the five brave little kings marched out of their cities and drew up their battle lines. They soon fled to the hills while Kedorlaomer and friends plundered their cities.

One of those cities was Sodom where Lot, Abraham's nephew, lived. When Abraham got the news, he called out 318 of his own men—servant warriors, perhaps—and set off in pursuit. He caught up with the kings

---

3. Josh 24:2.

4. Richard Allen, *Star Names*, 2

5. Gen 12:1–3.

150 miles later, at what is now Israel's northern border, attacked them and chased those who escaped one hundred miles further, recovering Lot and all the stolen people and possessions.

Melchizedek

When Abraham returned to Canaan, Melchizedek, king of Salem came to meet him. The name *Melchizedek* means "king of righteousness." Some think this was the aged Shem who had stood so long for righteousness.

Melchizedek brought bread and wine. He blessed Abraham and he blessed God who gave Abraham victory over his enemies. Abraham accepted Melchizedek's hospitality and blessing, and honored him by giving him a tenth of all he had.

The king of Sodom also came to meet Abraham. He offered all the plunder to Abraham, but Abraham refused it. He had sworn to God not to accept anything from the king lest the king boast that he had made Abraham rich. This incident puts Abraham clearly on the side of patriarchal authority under God and against kingship supported by idolatry and conquest.

Jacob

Abraham was one hundred years old when Isaac, the son God promised him, was born. Isaac fathered twin sons, Esau and Jacob. God chose Jacob, the younger, to carry on the promise. Jacob's life was complicated by intrigues—his own and others'—but he fathered twelve sons who became the patriarchs of the twelve tribes of Israel.[6]

Jacob's sons didn't get along well with each other. Joseph, next to the youngest, got the brunt of it—mainly because he was Jacob's favorite. One day Joseph reported to his father and brothers, "Listen, I had another dream, and this time the sun and moon and eleven stars were bowing down to me."

Jacob rebuked him. "What is this . . . ? Will your mother and I and your brothers actually come and bow down to the ground before you?" However, he kept this in mind.[7] Jacob recognized the sun and moon to be himself and his wife, and the eleven stars to be his sons. Perhaps these were not individual stars, but the twelve star groups of the zodiac. Judah for one had

---

6. God changed Jacob's name, which means *one who takes another by the heel (usurper)*, to Israel, which means *powerful with God*.

7. Gen 37:9–11.

an ensign at that time,[8] and later the tribes each displayed one of the zodiacal signs as its ensign.[9] Some people see allusions to the signs in blessings Jacob pronounced on his sons,[10] and those Moses pronounced on the tribes.[11] However, there is disagreement as to which tribe carried which sign.[12]

Joseph's jealous brothers sold him as a slave and led their father to believe that a wild animal killed him. Joseph ended up in Egypt where he rose in power to become next in command to Pharaoh. Because of famine in Canaan, Jacob moved his whole family to Egypt: seventy direct male descendants with their wives, daughters, daughters-in-law and servants. And in Egypt, they did indeed bow to Joseph.

David

The Israelites multiplied until the Egyptians became afraid of them and put them to slave labor. The Israelites cried to God and he sent Moses to lead them—now numbering about a million—out of Egypt and back to Canaan. They had been in Egypt 430 years.

With God's help the Israelites took their promised land from the Canaanites. But their dedication to God did not last long. During the next three hundred years the nation wavered between God and pagan religions. Finally, the people demanded a king so they could be like the nations around them whose kings led them in their wars.[13] The Prophet Samuel warned them that life under a king would mean heavy taxes and forced conscription, but they were adamant.

Their first king, Saul, fell to the temptations of all kings: he set up a monument to himself[14] and tried to serve as priest as well.[15] So God chose a new king, a young shepherd named David, the seventh son of his father.[16] In addition to his skill as a warrior, David was musical and poetical. He wrote that beautiful Psalm, "The LORD is my shepherd, I

8. Gen 38:18.

9. Num 2:2.

10. Gen 49.

11. Deut 33.

12. *Ensign* is the same word used in Genesis 1:14 for the stars serving as *signs*.

13. 1 Sam 8.

14. 1 Sam 15:12.

15. 1 Sam 13:6–14.

16. I Sam 16.

shall not be in want."[17] He would serve as a shepherd king under God, the Great Shepherd.

Some of David's Psalms mention the stars. Shepherding required him to be outside at night. He probably knew the night sky like the back of his hand. He wrote

> The heavens declare the glory of God;
> the skies proclaim the work of his hands.
> Day after day they pour forth speech;
> night after night they display knowledge.
> There is no speech or language
> where their voice is not heard.
> Their voice goes out into all the earth,
> their words to the ends of the world.[18]

Whatever David knew or didn't know of Adam's astronomy, he at least knew that the heavens did not praise false gods. Toward the end of his life, God promised David that Messiah, the Deliverer, would be one of his descendants.[19]

Solomon

David's son, Solomon, followed him as king. Solomon's wisdom brought him international fame. He received envoys from all over the world. But Solomon did not remain faithful to God. Solomon took hundreds of wives, amassed huge fortunes in gold and stabled large numbers of horses—the very things God had warned against.[20] He took wives from pagan nations, built temples for their gods, and joined them in burning incense and sacrificing.[21] When the kingdom split under Solomon's son, paganism was in to stay.

The northern ten tribes (Israel) suffered under many short-lived dynasties, every king a pagan. The kings of the southern two tribes (Judah), all from the line of David, managed only a few godly leaders. The people burned incense to the sun, moon and stars; baked raisin cakes for the Queen of Heaven; wept for Tammuz; and burned their own children in sacrifice to Moloch.

17. Ps 23:1.
18. Ps 19:1–4.
19. 2 Sam 7:16.
20. Deut 17:14–17.
21. 1 Kgs 11:1–8.

One prophet after another warned them, but apart from a tiny minority, they refused to listen. And so, God sent Assyria against Israel to kill and enslave them. Judah endured a little longer until Nebuchadnezzar, King of Babylon, did the same to them. God used foreign nations to punish his people just as he had used them to punish the Canaanites.

In spite of all, God did not forget his people. After all, the Deliverer must come from David's line. In seventy years, the prophets said, God will raise up a man named Cyrus who will issue a decree allowing the people of Judah to return and rebuild Jerusalem, their capital city.[22]

Daniel

Nebuchadnezzar's captives included many youths of the royal family and nobility. The good looking, intelligent and well educated ones were sent for special training.

Daniel and his friends Hananiah, Mishael, and Azariah determined to stay true to God. At the end of three years, all the trainees stood before the King to be tested. In every question Daniel and his friends beat out all the wise men of the kingdom. As a result, the king chose them for special service.

One night Nebuchadnezzar's dreams upset him. He called in his astrologers and magi and demanded that they tell him not only what his dream meant, but also the dream itself. Of course, none of them could, so the angry king ordered them all executed.

When the executioner came for him and his friends, Daniel asked for a chance to interpret the dream. Then he and his friends fasted and prayed.

Daniel's answer to the king was

> No wise man, enchanter, magician or diviner can explain to the king the mystery he has asked about, but there is a God in heaven who reveals mysteries. He has shown King Nebuchadnezzar what will happen in days to come.

And Daniel gave the dream and its meaning.[23]

The amazed king set Daniel as ruler over the entire province of Babylon and put him in charge of all the wise men. These men influenced Babylon, Babylon influenced the world, and Daniel had an open door for doing good.

22. Isa 44:28.
23. Dan 2:27–28.

Any of the Chaldeans (the Babylonian magi) who listened knew that neither Nimrod nor Ninus was the Deliverer, for Daniel certainly informed them of Balaam's prophecy that "A star will come out of Jacob; a scepter will rise out of Israel."[24] And he must have shared his vision about the future that revealed the time of Messiah's coming.[25]

Daniel was an old man when Cyrus conquered Babylon and set up the Persian Empire. Many captives returned to their homelands and, as God promised, Cyrus decreed the rebuilding of Jerusalem.[26]

The Magi

Four hundred years passed. Empires rose and fell just as Daniel had foretold. Mighty Rome swallowed up Greece, Phoenicia, and Egypt. Only Parthia resisted the Roman advance.

Perhaps in Susa, Parthia's summer capitol where Daniel had lived so long ago, or perhaps in Ctesiphon, the winter capital, some magi continued to wait for Daniel's Messiah. They knew to expect him about four hundred years after Daniel's time. They watched for the promised star, guided by God's spirit. The fact that they found the Christ child in this way is evidence that Adam's astronomy was not entirely forgotten, and that it indeed spoke of Messiah. One of the lessons of Daniel's life is that pagan wisdom can't measure up to the wisdom God supplies to those who wait on him.[27] The magi waited, and God led them.

Christianity

Those who recognized Jesus as the promised one, who saw him crucified and talked with him after his resurrection, understood that his blood paid their sin debt and that animal sacrifices were no longer needed. His resurrection proved he had satisfied God's righteousness and that they, too, would be resurrected. They proclaimed this good news to their fellow Jews and then to non-Jews (Gentiles) everywhere they went.

The early Church teacher Origen (185–254 AD) agreed with the Jewish historian Josephus that the constellations were known by Noah, Enoch, Seth and Adam, and mentioned in the *Book of Enoch* as "already

24. Num 24:17.
25. Dan 9:25–26.
26. Ezra 1:1–4.
27. Dan 1:18–20, 2:27–28, 5:13–17.

named and divided,"[28] but apparently no one attempted to separate Adam's astronomy from the pagan astrological signs—until the nineteenth century.

28. Richard Allen, *Star Names*, 27.

5

A British Lady to the Rescue

FOR CENTURIES in Europe, astronomy belonged to only a few people, such as scientists, mapmakers, and kings, but this changed in 1800 when the Royal Institution of London was established. Its purpose was to educate the public, and similar societies followed, including one for astronomy.

All this new knowledge excited a young British woman by the name of Frances Rolleston. She wanted to learn everything historical and scientific, especially astronomy. Frances believed the Bible's statement that the heavens show God's glory, yet the star maps cast the constellations as Greek gods and goddesses. Did the constellations once show God's glory? She devoted her life to answering that question.

Preparation

Frances was born to gentry in 1781. The Rolleston estate near Sherwood Forest had stood for three and a half centuries. Frances and her family visited the estate her father's brother had inherited, however, they lived near London. Frances hated the city, yet when she began researching her question, the British Museum and its wonderful library were right there.

When Frances was ten her mother died, and she was sent away for three years to relatives in Yorkshire—an old clergyman and his daughters. The Bible was already her favorite book, but now she became a true Christian, and immediately began sewing for the poor.[1] Here, also, she went to school for the first time. Until then she had only read with her mother. That doesn't mean she was ignorant—she was reading Shakespeare at age five.

When Frances returned from Yorkshire, she was ill for three years and studied little during that time. But at sixteen or seventeen, her desire to study reawakened through her tutor for French, English and poetry, and she

1. All the work Frances did during her life for poor people would fill a book. She established schools for poor children all over England, raising money, writing curriculum, teaching and training teachers.

began to do so in earnest. She took on Hebrew, which she continued all her life, Greek, Latin, Italian, and the natural history of plants and animals.

Next Frances tackled mathematical astronomy, French mathematics, and geology. She begged her father for a pair of globes, and memorized everything on them about the stars and constellations. Her understanding of astronomy was so good she taught it to a friend who was blind. Later, she wrote papers for the *Astronomical Register*, a journal for amateur observers.

The Quest

In 1811 at age thirty, Frances began looking for the answer to her question, researching the astronomical records of ancient nations. Twenty years later found her even more deeply involved in study. She would let her servant go to bed, take a fresh pair of candles and the celestial globe, and work from nine at night until three in the morning. After four years of that, her eyes gave her trouble, and she had to stop work at midnight.

If Frances had known only English, she could not have succeeded. Her many foreign languages, especially the ancient ones like Latin and Greek, enabled her to read very old astronomy books. In addition to learning the signs of various cultures, she found many ancient names of stars and constellations. Her goal was to determine the very earliest, believing these might be the names passed on through Noah.

The Method

Frances knew from the Bible that originally people spoke one language. She believed that the confusion of languages at Babel was a confusion of the *lip*, that is, pronunciation, as if everyone suddenly spoke with a strong foreign accent. (In Hebrew *lip* and *language* are the same word.)

Since the root words of Hebrew, Arabic, Chaldee and other ancient languages are similar, Frances believed them very close to Noah's language. She compared star names in various languages, picked out the roots and looked up the meanings in lexicons (dictionaries).

Parents often use baby name books to help them select a name. Sometimes they choose one for its meaning. Victor and Joy are English names we understand. Other names we use have meanings in Hebrew, Aramaic or Greek—the languages the Bible was written in. Stephen, for example, means *crown*. Deborah means *bee*. In the same way, star names have meanings in their languages, and these meanings, Frances believed, would lead to the message of the original constellations.

In modern astronomy books, meanings for star names frequently disagree with those Frances Rolleston gave. There are several reasons for this:

1. As various cultures developed, they often gave new names to the stars.

2. Over the millennia word spellings and meanings changed.

3. Pronunciation of a name in one language might sound like a word in another language. *Fair* means *lovely* in English, but the French *faire* means *to do* or *make.* An example of how this can confuse a researcher is Copernicus' (Polish astronomer, 1473–1543) belief that the star Regulus in the constellation Leo referred to Heaven's Guardian who *regulated* all things in the heavens. However, it really came from the Hebrew word *regel,* meaning *foot* (*rigel* in Arabic), because Leo represented the one who would trample the enemy under his foot.

4. Other star enthusiasts didn't understand her method of working from the angle of language. Richard Hinckley Allen, for example, in his *Star Names Their Lore and Meaning,* published in 1899, grouped her work with previous Christian and Jewish efforts to *recreate* the constellations as Biblical or moral images.[2]

Pictures, Please

The star names helped Frances understand the message of the signs, but she knew that if she could find the original pictures as well, she'd understand the message even better.

A breakthrough came with the French army in Egypt. A circular planisphere discovered inside the great temple at Dendera was removed and brought back to France. A friend gave Frances a lithograph of this planisphere.

It took a while for her to read it because first she had to learn Egyptian hieroglyphics. That was the hardest work she had ever done, and she was well into her seventies. She stuck to it because she knew the Greeks got their astronomy from Egypt, and therefore the Egyptian pictures were probably closer to the originals.

2. Richard Allen, *Star Names,* 28.

Some claim that the Dendera Zodiac actually dates from only a few years BC and some of its images are of Greek and other origin. However, the images were different from those previously available to Frances, and so the zodiac was still valuable to her. Adam and Enoch only imagined the figures on the sky. They didn't engrave them there. And so there is much room for variation in form. By seeing differing pictures, the commonality among them pointed out the original message.

A good example is Libra, portrayed as a woman holding a scales, a human figure lifting a scales in one hand and holding a lamb in the other, the scales alone, or a mounded dirt altar. All these point to God's justice and the need for a redeemer—someone to pay the penalty for sin.

The Scriptures

Frances searched the scriptures for occurrences of every star and constellation name. For the original astronomy to be God's message, it had to agree with his word. The scripture references in Frances' notes affirm the ideas behind the names and pictures. Her familiarity with the Bible enabled her to associate planisphere images with Biblical ones. For example, the Egyptian planisphere contained images that were part human and part animal, such as a man with a hawk's head. These she found similar to the "living creatures" in Ezekiel 1 and Revelation 4, which she believed symbolic of the divine joined to the human in the person of Messiah.

Challenges

Frances faced several difficulties in her work.

- Lack of money. She wrote, "I am resolving to print my Astronomy a sheet at a time, as I can afford it."[3] Back then the writer had to pay the publisher. In spite of being born into gentry, Frances did not have much money. The problem was that she was always giving her money away—to the schools she established for poor children and to victims of famine and war.

- Poor eyesight. Computers didn't exist; everything had to be written by hand. And because her eyesight was bad, Frances either put her paper on a tall stack of books to get it closer to her eyes, or held it against a piece of cardboard in front of her face.

3. Frances Rolleston to Cary Dent, June 17, 1853, in *Letters of Miss Frances Rolleston*, ed. Caroline Dent (London: Rivingtons, 1867) 341.

- Health problems. The flu attacked Frances almost every winter. Sometimes it was so bad she feared she might not live long enough to finish her work on the constellations.

Results

At last most of the work was finished and published in installments. Frances wrote that it took her fifty-five years' study to get her facts together, ten of them off and on at the reading room of the British Museum. But she continued to study, wanting to know more about the astronomy of India.

The year after her death at almost 83 years of age, her notes were gathered into one book, *Mazzaroth: The Constellations*. She left money in her will for a friend to publish it for her.[4]

One of the people interested in Frances's research was Ethelbert W. Bullinger. He and Frances corresponded about her discoveries. He organized her work into a book of his own, *The Witness of the Stars*, published in 1893. His was much easier to read than hers. In America, Joseph A. Seiss studied Frances' notes, and in 1882 he published *The Gospel in the Stars*.

Most scholars, however, ignored *Mazzaroth*. Few scholars or church leaders in England at the time had a strong belief in the Bible. Frances' work showed that truths of God's word were known even before the Bible was written—strong evidence for the Bible's trustworthiness, and something they perhaps preferred not to consider.

This is not to claim that everything Frances Rolleston wrote was accurate. Discoveries have been made since her time, and she did make mistakes. But it is reasonable that she was correct about a God-honoring astronomy that predated paganism.

4. Frances Rolleston, will dated December 2, 1863, proved June 27, 1864, Cumbria Record Office, Whitehaven, UK.

6

The Story in the Stars

IF THE story in the stars sounds familiar—like the model for all tales of adventure and romance—it's no wonder, for it is the greatest, truest story ever. God himself is the author. It was not invented by the Jewish people nor by Christians. God told it to the first humans long before any formal religion existed. In the following rendition, the Great King represents God; the king's son is Messiah, the Deliverer; and the princess is all those who love him.

The Story

The Great King of the Universe seeks a bride for his son, and settles upon a princess of excellence. The prince is pleased with his father's choice, but the situation is complicated when the princess defies the Great King. The prince must do more than win her affection, for her crime has enslaved her to a cruel master who holds the power of death. Her life is forfeit unless someone—someone without guilt of his own—dies in her place.

The prince would gladly lay down his life for the one he loves. His purity qualifies him. But there is an impediment: he is immortal. Determined to do his utmost, he takes on human form and dies in her place. His sacrifice pleases the Great King, who not only raises him from the dead, but declares him Crown Prince.

Will the princess fall in love with the one who gave his life for her? Will she accept his hand and his kingdom? She does! They are betrothed, and await the happy day.

A time of testing follows. The Prince must leave to prepare a home for his bride. Knowing that the enemy will seek revenge for the loss of his slave, the Prince provides her with armor and gifts of wisdom to defend herself until his return. The enemy's tactic of deceit enables him to kill and destroy. But he cannot win in the end. The Prince returns to utterly destroy him and his power, and to be crowned King of kings and Lord of lords. He and his bride reign forever.

Storybook in the Stars

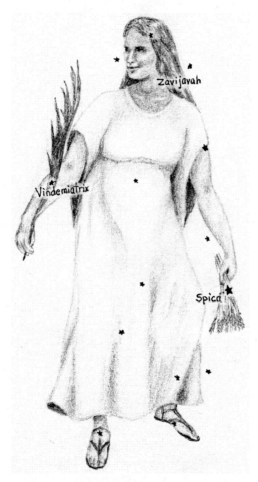

Virgo

Here is the woman, mother of the human race,[1] representative of all who come after her. She is the princess of the story, the one who tasted the fruit of rebellion, and the one to whom God pledged his love by promising a Deliverer.

She stands holding grain in one hand and a branch in the other. These represent her coming deliverer. Her brightest star, Spica, *ear of corn,* marks the promised Seed. Vindemiatrix, *the son or branch who comes,*[2] points out the branch. The woman's name is Virgo, the *virgin,* bearer of the promised Deliverer.[3]

1. Gen 3:20.
2. Zech 3:8.
3. The names and meanings of the constellations and stars are presented in greater

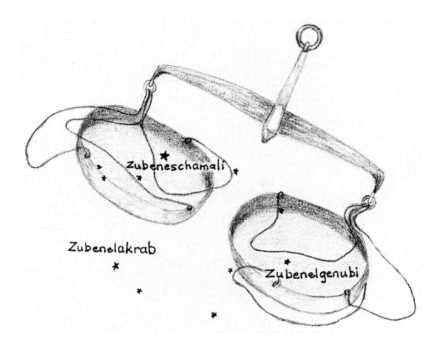

Libra.

The circle of stars suggests the original circular altar. The altar[4] is needed because the woman cannot free herself from the penalty of her rebellion. All her efforts weigh in as *price deficient* (Zubenalgenubi).[5] The Deliverer, however, will provide *the price which covers* (Zubeneschamali).[6]

---

detail in Appendix A.

4. Exod 20:24–26.

5. Ps 49:7–8; 62:9.

6. 1 Cor 6:20; 1 Pet 1:18–19.

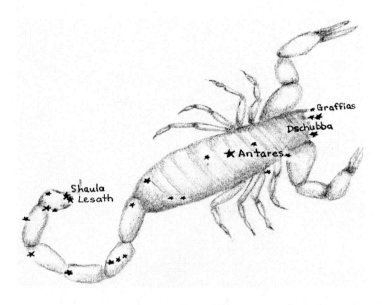

Scorpius

Scorpius, *scorpion*,[7] enemy of God and of the human race, wields a fear-some *sting* (Shaula).[8]

7. Ps 91:13.
8. Prov 23:32; 1 Cor 15:55–56.

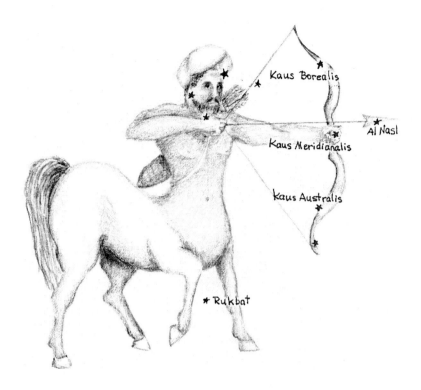

Sagittarius

The *archer who sends forth the arrow,* takes the field.[9] He aims at Antares, the enemy's heart, already named *wounding* because this archer cannot fail.

9. Ps 45:4-5.

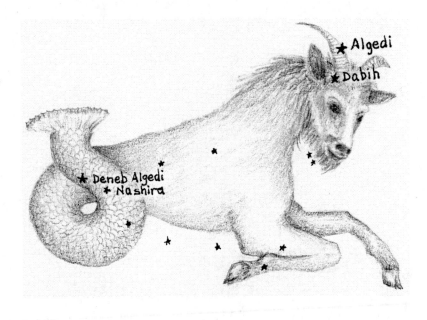

Capricornus

In the battle the Deliverer lays down his life[10] as *the goat* (Capricornus), the *sacrifice slain* (Dabih).[11] Capricornus' ancient name, Hupenius, means *place of bearing*, because Messiah bore the sins of others, not his own.[12] His sacrifice is not defeat; it brings new life for many—shown by the lively fish tail.[13]

10. John 10:17–18.

11. Exod 12:5.

12. 1 Pet 2:21–24.

13. Fish often signify God's people, an idea carried over into the Christian sign of the fish; Mark 1:16–17.

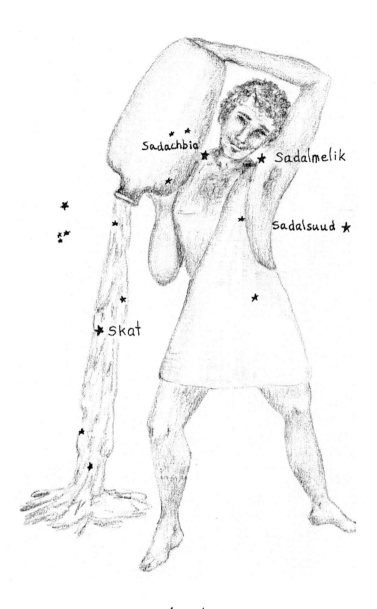

Aquarius
The Deliverer now appears *rising up, pouring forth water* (Aquarius) on his
people—the gift of the Holy Spirit.[14]

14. John 7:37–39; Ezek 47:1–12.

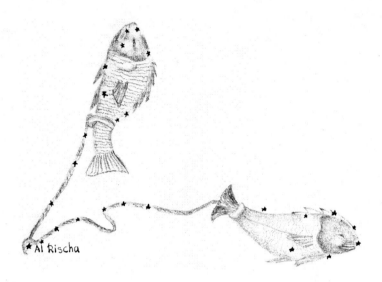

Pisces

The message of life spreads throughout the world. People from north and south, east and west,[15] *multiplying as fish* (Pisces), are united by The Band.[16]

15. Ps 107:2–3; John 10:16; Eph 2:11–18.
16. Hos 11:4.

Aries.

Aries is often drawn with head bowed, as the stars seem to suggest. Though once the *bruised one* (Sheratan), Aries, *the ram or lamb*, stands triumphant.[17]

17. John 1:29; Rev 5:6.

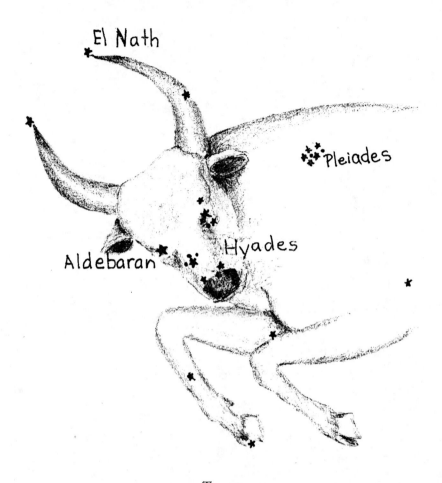

Taurus

Then like a great *bull* (Taurus), he comes to reign.[18] Bringing his people The Pleiades and The Hyades[19] with him, he takes his place as Aldebaran, the *leader, governor.*[20]

18. Deut 33:17.
19. See Chapter 7, item 26.
20. Isa 9:7; Gen 49:10.

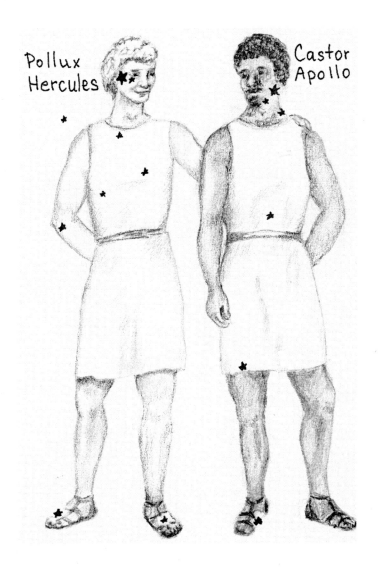

Gemini

Who is this leader? The One with two natures *united* (Gemini)—both God and man,[21] immortal Pollux and mortal Castor, *sufferer* (Hercules)[22] and *judge* (Apollo).

21. Phil 2:6–7.
22. 1 Pet 4:1.

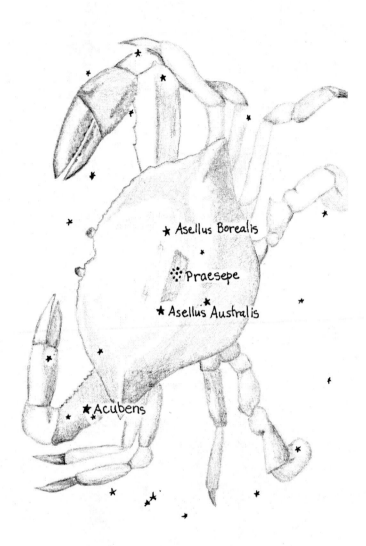

Cancer.

The circle of stars outlines the original cattle fold. The Deliverer *encircles* (Cancer) the *multitude* of his people (Praesepe),[23] making *a hiding place* (Acubens) for them.[24] The place of safety is required because judgment now falls upon the earth.

23. Ps 107:32.
24. Ps 91:1; Ps 27:1–6.

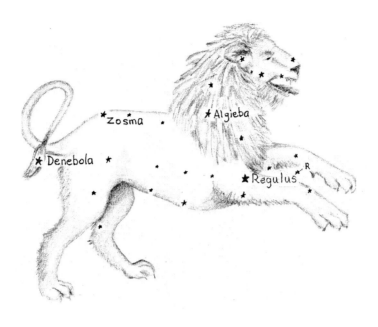

Leo

As a ferocious *lion* (Leo) the *judge quickly comes* (Denebola) to *tread* his enemies *underfoot* (Regel).[25]

25. Gen 49:9; Rev 5:5; Prov 19:12.

Glorious Astronomy Facts

A METEOR shower is a fun and easy sky watching treat. People have good reason for calling those bright streaks "shooting stars." All that's needed is a lawn chair and a dark sky, away from street lights, porch lights and brightly lit windows.

Though meteors appear all over the sky, those of a shower appear to originate in one small area of the sky. Observers call this spot the *radiant*. The related word *radiance* means a quality of being brilliant, as in "The Son is the *radiance* of God's glory."[1] Almost all showers radiate from constellations picturing the Deliverer, his people, or his glory.

Aquarius, picturing the Deliverer pouring water, has five meteor showers—a lovely image of abundant blessing that accords with the Bible theme of "former and latter rains."[2] In Palestine, to receive both the former and latter rain was a sign of God's blessing. The Old Testament prophets used the former and latter rains to picture Messiah's coming.[3] In the New Testament, the image refers to Messiah's second coming.[4]

The Ursids and Pisces-Australids represent Messiah's *reflected* glory, since they radiate from constellations picturing the people God adopted "to the praise of his glorious grace."[5] Some day we will shine like the stars.[6]

This table lists the better meteor showers. The number of meteors per hour is only approximate since the number can vary greatly from year to year, and also depends on viewing conditions.

1. Heb 1:3
2. Deut 11:14.
3. Hos 6:3.
4. Jas 5:7.
5. Eph 1:5–6.
6. Dan 12:3; Matt 13:43; Phil 2:15.

Meteor Showers

Shower Name	Constellation	Maximum Activity Date	Maximum Number of Meteors Per Hour
Quadratids	Boötes	January 3–4	120
Lyrids	Lyra	April 22	18
Eta Aquarids	Aquarius	May 6	60
June Bootids	Boötes	June 27	0–100
Delta Aquarids	Aquarius	July 28	20
Perseids	Perseus	August 12–13	70
Orionids	Orion	October 21	23
Leonids	Leo	November 17	10–100
Geminids	Gemini	December 14	120
Ursids	Ursa Minor	December 22	10

Meteors are not the only objects in the sky with meaning. Stars and other objects also confirm God's message.

1. The most important star in Virgo, the *virgin* who bears the branch, is Spica, the Branch, a blue and white eclipsing binary. As a double it shows that the Branch has two natures—God and man. For the short while that he was on earth, Messiah's godhood was eclipsed by his humanity.

Spica is only about twice the size of the Sun, but its luminosity exceeds the Sun's more than 2,000 times. Messiah the Branch, though appearing like an ordinary man, is actually the "radiance of God's glory."

2. Coma, *the desired one*, pictured as the child on the virgin's lap, tells of Messiah's birth. The stars that form the constellation are not remarkable to look at. None are bright. And neither was the coming of the Desired One. Born in a stable to simple people, his birth would have passed unnoticed apart from some shepherds who heard the angels' announcement and the magi who were watching for it. However, larger telescopes reveal that beyond Coma's dim stars, running through both Virgo and Coma, is a remarkable region containing dozens of bright galaxies. Just so, beneath the common appearance of the Desired One resides divine glory.

3. In Centaurus, *the despised centaur*, shines Rigel Kentaurus, the third brightest star in the sky. It is a triple system of the three stars closest to us—significant if we think of it as representing the Trinity reaching out to mankind. The closest, Proxima Centauri, is a red dwarf whose color reminds us that the Deliverer, second person of the Trinity, came all the way to earth to shed his blood for our redemption.

4. Boötes, *plowman, coming*, features one of the finest collections of double stars. The large number of doubles emphasizes the fact that the Deliverer comes for more than one purpose. The blue and orange Izar, *the preserver*, shows he comes to guard his people. The blue-white Alkalurops, *treading underfoot*, speaks his purpose toward his enemies.

5. Libra, *The Scales*, has a noted shell star, 48 Librae. Its outer atmosphere, or shell, may be dormant for many years and then suddenly become active. Rotating at exceptional velocity, its equatorial ring of gases—about twice the star's diameter—expands swiftly.

On one side of the scales, evil may appear small or dormant, but when it flares up it has far-reaching consequences.[7] Death entered the world through one man and spread to all.[8] On the other side of the scales, the promise of a deliverer seemed dormant for thousands of years, but its fulfillment has meant salvation to millions.[9]

6. Crux, *Cutting Off*, tells about the central event of history. In addition to the cross itself, formed by four bright stars, several features portray that event.

- Below the right arm of the cross (left side as we look at it from the northern hemisphere) is the largest dark nebula visible to the

7. Jas 1:15; 3:5.

8. Rom 5:12.

9. Rom 5:18–19.

unaided eye. The Coal Sack pictures our load of sin, for "he himself bore our sins in his body on the tree."[10]

- If we imagine a figure on the cross, the variable star Epsilon Crucis at his side portrays the mixed blood and water that issued from where a right-handed soldier would likely thrust his spear.[11]

- At the right hand of the cross glitters the Jewel Box (NGC 4755). About 50 of its 100 stars are colorful supergiants in reds, blues, yellows and whites. Many have very high luminosities, approaching 100,000 Suns. We are jewels in the Deliverer's right hand,[12] the treasure Messiah died to gain.[13]

- Crux has four beta CMa type variables (also called beta Cephei stars). These very hot giants pulsate. Their throbbing power reminds us that "the message of the cross is foolishness to those who are perishing, but to us who are being saved it is the power of God."[14]

7. Lupus, *the Victim*, is inconspicuous, having no very bright stars. Isaiah prophesied that the rejected Messiah would not be remarkable to look at.[15] However, Lupus lies on the Milky Way, and therefore behind it are many lovely stars, including an unusual proportion of doubles. "In [him] are hidden all the treasures of wisdom and knowledge."[16]

8. Corona Borealis, *the Northern Crown*, is an almost perfect semi-circle of jewel-like stars, including many variables and doubles. Alphecca, a brilliant white jewel in the crown, is near the radiant of the Coronid meteor showers. The crown speaks to us of the Deliverer's glory which will shower upon us.

R Coronae Borealis is a nova in reverse. Every few years it goes through catastrophic changes and becomes dim, perhaps due to sooty carbon particles in its outer layers. It speaks to us of another crown, stained with dark drops of blood, that preceded the crown of glory.[17]

---

10. 1 Pet 2:24.

11. John 19:33–37.

12. Rev 1:16.

13. *Treasure* Mal 3:16–17 NIV, *jewels* in the AV.

14. 1 Cor 1:18.

15. Isa 53:2–3.

16. Col 2:3.

17. John 19:2.

9. In Scorpius, the supergiant Antares—also called Heart of the Scorpion—burns orange-red, illuminating a pale red nebula. The nebula's eerie glow spreads over a large region, like a veil of evil over the earth.

The scorpion's tail overlies rich Milky Way star clouds, but the stars are dimmed and obscured by dark dust. Similarly, evil may tarnish God's good gifts.

NGC 6231 is an open cluster of supergiants that resemble the Pleiades in miniature. If the two clusters were the same distance, NGC 6231 would shine 50 times brighter than the Pleiades. Since the Pleiades represent God's people (see Taurus), NGC 6231 in Scorpius may be represent devilish impostors.

10. A triangle of three bright stars forms the head of Serpens, *the Accursed*. Between two of these, where one might imagine the creature's throat, a Mira variable suggests the deceptive speech of the "father of lies."[18]

11. Ophiuchus, *Holder of the Serpent*, struggles with the enemy on our behalf. Rho Ophiuchi, a complex multiple star, lies in the foot with which Ophiuchus crushes Scorpius. The region around Rho Ophiuchi contains several dark nebulae, reminding us that crushing the enemy meant blood and pain for the Deliver. The dark nebulae may also remind us of the darkness that came at noon when he hung on the cross.[19]

12. In Hercules, *The Strong*, M13 (NGC 6205) appears to the naked eye as a fuzzy spot. But this very compact spectacular globular cluster, considered the best in the northern hemisphere, contains over a million stars. It lies on Hercules' thigh. "On his robe and on his thigh he has this name written: King of kings and Lord of lords."[20]

13. Toward the center of the Milky Way, Sagittarius, *the archer*, rides to glorious victory across rich star fields. Numerous clusters and nebulae appear within the constellation, three of which are the Lagoon Nebula (NGC 6523), the Omega Nebula (NGC 6618), and The Trifid Nebula (NGC 6514).

14. Though otherwise small and faint, Lyra, *the harp*, is home to the fifth brightest star, Vega, *he shall be praised*. This star dominates the summer skies in the northern hemisphere, and forms part of the summer triangle with the bright stars Altair, *wounding*, and Deneb, *judge*. All three stars are in constellations pictured as birds, and they summarize the

18. John 8:44.
19. Luke 23:44–45.
20. Rev 19:16.

Deliverer's story: Aquila, *the wounded eagle*, speaks of his death on our behalf; Cygnus, the swan *who goes and returns*, his return as judge; and Lyra, the eagle bearing a *harp*, the praise he will receive.

15. Constellations take on a slightly different appearance depending on the time of year or the time of night. When Beta and Gamma are at the top of Draco's head, they look like two eyes, or perhaps the forehead. At other times the face is indistinct. Our enemy's appearance changes, too. He is able to disguise himself as an angel of light and work by hiding his true character.[21]

16. Capricornus, *Sacrifice Slain*. M30 (NGC 7099) is a globular cluster with a very concentrated center. From this center to the periphery stretches a number of star chains (or strings). "Bind the sacrifice with cords, even unto the horns of the altar."[22]

17. In Aquila, *the wounded eagle*, the principal star, Altair, spins very rapidly. This spinning deforms Altair until its equatorial diameter is thought to be twice its polar diameter. In his *wounding*, Messiah was marred and disfigured more than any man.[23]

18. A remarkable star in Aquarius, *pouring forth of water*, is R Aquarii, usually listed as a Mira variable. However, it isn't a normal variable; it's a symbiotic star—a binary system of two different temperatures. The red giant is cooler than its very hot small blue companion. The Bearer of the water of life wants those on whom he pours his Spirit be cold or hot, not lukewarm.[24]

19. Cygnus, *who goes and returns*, has three significant stars.

- Astronomer David Levy calls Deneb, *judge*, "one of the mightiest stars known—25 times more massive and 60,000 times more luminous than the Sun."[25] The Deliverer's return will be "in power and great glory."[26]

21. 2 Cor 11:13–15.
22. Ps 118:27 AV.
23. Isa 52:14.
24. Rev 3:15–16.
25. David Levy, *Skywatching*, 164.
26. Matt 24:30.

- Cygnus A is the second brightest source in the radio sky. Two lobes of radio emission are fed by jets of energetic particles from the galaxy core[27]—another reminder of his return in power.

- NGC 686, the Blinking Nebula has a fairly bright star at its center. If you concentrate on the star, the surrounding nebula disappears; if you concentrate on the nebula, the star disappears. The Apostle Paul wrote that at the Lord's return, we will be changed "in a flash, in the twinkling of an eye."[28]

20. Even the brightest galaxy in Pisces, *the Fishes*, is faint. God chose his people for no brightness of their own, but simply because of his love for them.[29] A poetic description of Jerusalem as an orphaned infant illustrates God's choosing and their dependency: "Then I passed by and saw you kicking about in your blood, and as you lay there in your blood I said to you, 'Live!'"[30] The exceptionally deep red star TX Psc is reminiscent of blood.

21. Andromeda, *the Chained Woman*, is probably best known for M31, The Andromeda Galaxy. It can be seen with the naked eye under dark skies as a hazy smudge. Long-exposure photographs show that its spiral arms span the sky six times the width of the full Moon, recalling the great length God went to to free us from our chains.

22. When men first studied the heavens, the Sun passed through Aries, *the Ram*, at the vernal equinox. The vernal equinox has now moved into Pisces, but is still known as the First Point of Aries. The first point of God's eternal plan of redemption was "the Lamb that was slain from the creation of the world."[31]

23. Cassiopeia, *the Enthroned Woman*, was once a captive in chains (pictured in Andromeda). The stars of her open cluster NGC 457 appear to be arranged in chains. These chains lie to the woman's left, near the sword of Perseus, her deliverer.

24. In Cetus, the Monster, lies Mira (Omicron Cetir), one of the earliest discovered variables and the prototype of long period variables. This ever-changing red star in the monster's throat points out the enemy's lies.

---

27. See Philip Blanco's web page devoted to Cygnus A, http://mamacass.ucsd.edu/people/pblanco/cyga.html.

28. 1 Cor 15:52.

29. Deut 7:6–8.

30. Ezek 16:6.

31. Rev 13:8.

25. Perseus, *the Breaker*, carries a severed head. In the head is a bright white eclipsing binary, the star Algol, *the evil spirit*. Its A and B components are orbited by a third. Here is the false trinity, the dragon and two beasts of Revelation 13. The eclipse comes about every 3 *days* and lasts 10 *hours*. The orbit of C is about 2 *years*. The red giant Rho Persei, also in the demon's head, fluctuates approximately every *month*. The *hours, days, months* and *years* of Algol and Rho Persei remind us that the enemy is constantly seeking someone to devour.[32]

26. Taurus, *coming, ruling*, has two interesting open star clusters which represent God's people. The Hyades forms the face of the bull. "Thou . . . settest me before thy face for ever."[33] Nine of the dozen visible stars of The Hyades and the seven visible stars of The Pleiades have personal names: "Rejoice that your names are written in heaven."[34]

The Pleiades, *congregation of the ruler*,[35] appears as a slightly hazy group of about six stars carried on the bull's shoulder. It actually contains hundreds of stars (some say thousands) spread over an area four times the size of the full Moon. Long-exposure photographs show that the whole cluster is enveloped in a faint nebulus—a lovely picture of the "robe of righteousness" with which God clothes his people.[36]

27. Orion, *light coming forth*, is true to the meaning of its name. It is full of breathtaking light-bearers, from the red supergiant Betelgeuse and blue-white supergiant Rigel (seventh brightest star in the sky), to the three stars which form the famous belt. The Great Nebula, visible to the naked eye as a fuzzy patch, is a vast complex of twisted and swirling gas and dust, exquisitely lit by surrounding stars.[37] Orion's belt recalls two scripture images: the sash the priests wore "to give them dignity and honor,[38] and the golden sash from John's vision of the risen Christ.[39]

28. When Messiah miraculously fed the 5,000, he had the people recline in groups of hundreds and fifties.[40] Three star clusters in Auriga the

---

32. 1 Pet 5:8.
33. Ps 41:12 AV.
34. Luke 10:20.
35. Ps 22:22.
36. Isa 61:10; Eph 4:22–24.
37. 1 John 1:5; John 8:12.
38. Exod 28.40.
39. Rev 1:13.
40. Mark 6:39–40.

Shepherd remind us of that event: M36 has about 50 stars, M38 about 100, and M37 perhaps 150. Within M37, twelve red giants, with the brightest one at their center, makes a lovely picture of the apostles serving among those clustered around the Lord.

29. Pollux, *the servant*, is the larger and brighter of the Gemini twins, but Castor, *the lord*, is richer. Castor actually consists of three stars—two blue-whites around which a red dwarf slowly revolves. As though to confirm Messiah's dual nature, each of these is itself a double, so that Castor actually consists of six stars.

30. Since Orion claims so much attention, nearby Lepus, *enemy*, is often ignored. The enemy of our souls doesn't mind that he can go about his work unnoticed and unhindered. The fact that Lepus is nondescript, that is, portrayed as no particular animal, suggests Satan's many disguises.

31. The brightest star in the sky, Sirius, *the Prince*, has a very dim, very close companion called The Pup. This white dwarf is about twice the size of Earth, but its mass nearly equals the Sun's. A tablespoonful of its matter would weigh over a ton. Our Prince calls us his friends[41] and to him we have infinite weight and value.

32. In Cancer, *Encircling*, God's people—his possession—are pictured by M44, the Beehive Cluster. At least 100 of its 300 stars are brighter than our sun. The Bible says that some day God's people will shine like the sun and stars. The cluster is visible to the naked eye on a dark enough night. May God's people also shine brighter in the surrounding darkness.

33. Ursa Minor, Lesser Flock. The present pole star is located at the very end of Ursae Minoris, and around it all the stars of the sky appear to rotate. God's flock is the focus of heaven's activity. Several thousand years ago, there was a different pole star. The sky appeared to revolve around Thuban, *the Subtle*, at the time Nimrod's false religion was spreading out from Babel.

34. In Argo the ship, both Puppis and Carina lie over the Milky Way. These are the stern and lower part of the ship where travelers might rest. Within them, numerous open clusters picture the multitudes who fill Messiah's kingdom. Vela, *the sail*, is graced with a huge supernova remnant that covers sixteen times the moon's width of the sky and easily suggests a billowing sail.

41. John 15:15.

35. Leo, *the Lion Rending*, contains a reminder that he is the same person who gave his life for us. When his disciples saw the resurrected Messiah, he told them to look at the wounds in his hands and feet.[42] Leo's forepaw bears the mark. There, R Leonis, one of the brightest, most easily observed Mira variables, becomes extremely bright every 312 days. Deep red, approaching purple, its color is even more pronounced next to the white stars around it. One observer reported: "It looks stunningly deep reddish purple (crimson?), like a ruby or a grape or an opened heart."[43]

36. Hydra, *the Serpent*, slithers below Libra, Virgo, Leo and Cancer—across 100 degrees of sky. Near its center, an eerie, greenish-blue eye, known as The Eye Nebula (NGC 3242), glows small and bright, a blue dwarf as the pupil. Because this nebula slightly resembles Jupiter, it's also called The Ghost of Jupiter. Ancient astronomy recognized Jupiter as the king planet, and how greatly the serpent desires to be king!

37. Corvus, *the Raven*, bird of punishment,[44] *ravenously* tears Hydra's flesh. Two unusual galaxies in Corvus illustrate that tearing. NGC 4038 (the Ringtale Galaxy), a rare type classified as "peculiar," resembles a foetus. NGC 4027 appears faint and disturbed.

The early patriarchs probably did not see the objects described here. Perhaps God created them with us and our magnificent telescopes in mind. And why not, since he included us in his plan? The end of the story is yet to happen, and our part in it depends on whether we are standing faithful to him or following a religion that excludes him.

Glossary for Chapter Seven

binaries. If a star is actually two stars revolving around each other, it is a binary. In some binaries one star passes in front so the other cannot be seen for a period of time. This is called an eclipsing binary.

clusters. Star groups range from tens to hundreds of thousands of stars. Open clusters have only tens or hundreds of members, and these can be picked out individually. They are also called galactic clusters because they are within our own galaxy. Globular clusters

42. Luke 24:39.
43. Ron Bhanukitsiri, "TV-102 performed open-heart surgery on Lion."
44. Prov 30:17.

look like fuzzy balls in smaller telescopes, but larger telescopes show that each of these balls contains many thousands of stars.

doubles. Stars close enough together to appear as one are called *doubles*. Some doubles are optical only; that is, the stars aren't actually near each other but only appear so in our line of vision. Sometimes a double or binary turns out to be more than two stars since one or more of them may also be doubles.

galaxies. Galaxies contain perhaps 100 billion stars gathered in a spiral, elliptical or irregular mass. Galaxies may appear in clusters and even superclusters.

nebulae. Nebulae are clouds of gas and dust which may be bright or dark, depending on whether they are lit by stars (within or nearby), or whether they blot out the stars behind them.

novae. A nova is a star which flares with a huge increase in brightness for a few days or months. Some have been known to repeat this flare-up after many years and are known as recurrent novae.

star types. The many types of stars range widely in size, temperature, color, brightness and mass—from the red dwarf and neutron stars, through the yellow main sequence types, to the hot blue and cool red giants, and the rare supergiants. They maybe as small as the earth or a thousand times the size of the sun. Small stars can have tremendous mass.

variables. These stars vary in brightness. An eclipsing binary becomes dimmer as one member eclipses the other, then brighter as the dimmer member moves aside. Mira stars are red giants that slowly pulsate. It takes some hundreds of days to become brighter then dimmer. Cepheids take only a day or more to expand which causes them to become dimmer, and then to shrink, becoming brighter. They do this at regular intervals.

Appendix A

Table of Star and Constellation Name Meanings

IN THIS table, each of the twelve zodiacal signs is followed by three de-cans (companion constellations) and is limited to two stars each. Many more stars can be found in the books mentioned at the end of Chapter 5. The stars are identified by their Bayer letters to help locate them on modern star maps. Star location within the constellation picture often adds to the meaning.

Sign or Decan	Other Names or Meanings	Figure	Bayer Letter and Location	Ancient Name, Meaning	Other Names, Meanings
1 Virgo = virgin	Virgin, branch similar in Heb, Latin, Arabic	Woman with branch, stalks of grain	Alpha Virginis in left hand	Spica = ear of corn	Al Zimach = branch
			Eta Virginis in right arm	Vindemiatrix = son, branch who comes	
Coma Berenices = Berenice's Hair	Coma = the desired, longed for	Woman seated hold-ing child			
Centaurus = centaur	Bezeh = the despised	Centaur holding spear	Alpha Centauri in left front foot	Rigil Kentaurus = foot of the centaur	Cheiron = the pierced
			Beta Centauri in right front foot	Hadar = honor, majesty	
Boötes = plowman	Bau = to come	Man walking fast with branch, sickle	Alpha Boötis in left knee	Arcturus	Arktouros = keeper of the bear
			Beta Boötis in head	Nekkar = the pierced	

59

2 Libra = scales	Al Zubena = purchase, redemption	Scales	Alpha Librae in left side	Zubenalgenubi = price deficient	
			Beta Librae in right side	Zubeneschamali = price which covers	
Crux = cross	Adom = cutting off	Cross		none	
Lupus = wolf	Asedah = to be slain	Animal		none	
Corona Borealis = northern crown	Atarah = kingly crown; Al Iclil = jewel	Crown	Alpha Coronae Borealis right of center	Gemma	Al Phecca = the shining
3 Scorpius = scorpion	Isidis = attack of the enemy	Scorpion	Alpha Scorpii in heart	Antares (Arab) = wounding	
			Lambda Scorpii in tail	Shaula = the sting	Lesath = the perverse
Serpens = serpent	Alyah = the accursed	Serpent	Alpha Serpentis in center of upper half	Unukalhai = encompassing the reptile	
			Beta Serpentis in throat		Cheleb, Chelbalrai = serpent enfolding
Ophiuchus = holder of the serpent	Afeichus = serpent held	Man grasping serpent, treading scorpion	Alpha Ophiuchi in head	Ras Alhague = head of him who holds	
			Theta Ophiuchi [?] in foot		Saiph = bruised
Hercules = the strong	El Giscale = the strong	Man on one knee holding branch, monster head	Alpha Herculis in head	Ras Algethi = head of him who bruises	
			Beta Herculis in shoulder		Kornephorus = branch kneeling

4 Sagittarius = archer who sends forth arrow	Archer, bow, arrow	Centaur, bow, arrow pointed at scorpion's heart	Alpha Sagittarii between front legs	Rukbat = riding of bowman	
			Gamma Sagittarii in arrow	Al Nasl = the point	
Lyra = lyre, harp		Lyre or eagle holding lyre	Alpha Lyrae	Vega = he shall be exalted	
			Beta Lyrae	Sheliak = eagle	
Ara = altar	Al Mugamra = finishing	Altar with fire		none	
Draco = dragon		Long serpent or dragon	Alpha Draconis near tail	Thuban = the subtle	
			Beta Draconis in head	Rastaban = dragon's head	
5 Capricornus = goat	Hupenius = place of bearing	Goat bowing down, lively fish tail	Alpha Capricorni in head	Algedi = the kid, cut down	
			Beta Capricorni in head	Dabih = sacri- fice slain	
Sagitta = arrow	Scham = destroying	Arrow		none	
Aquila = eagle	Tarared = wounded	Eagle falling	Alpha Aquilae in throat or breast	Altair = the wounding	
			Beta Aquilae in head	Alshain = bright, scarlet	
Delphinus = dolphin	Dalaph = pouring out water	Dolphin. Vessel pouring (Egyptian)	Alpha Delphini in head	Sualocin = swift (as flow of water)	
			Beta Delphini in head	Rotanev = swiftly running	

6 Aquarius = rising up, pouring water	Deli = water urn. Hupei Tirion = place of pouring out	Man pouring water from urn	Alpha Aquarii in shoulder	Sadalmelik = blessed of the king	
			Beta Aquarii in other shoulder	Sadalsuud = the out pourer	
Piscus Austrinus = southern fish		Fish drinking waters from urn	Alpha Piscus Austrini	Formalhaut = fish's mouth	
Pegasus = coming quickly, joyfully		Winged horse	Alpha Pegasi in shoulder	Markab = returning from afar	
			Beta Pegasi in foreleg	Scheat = who goes and returns	
Cygnus = who circles	Azel = who goes, returns	Swan	Alpha Cygni in belly	Deneb = judge	
			Beta Cygni in head	Albireo = flying quickly	
7 Pisces = fish, multiplying	Dagim = fishes, multitude	Two fish held together by band	[?]	Okda = the united	
The Band (now part of Pisces)	Al Risha = the band, bridle	Cord or band uniting the fish	Alpha Piscium at base of cord	Al Risha = band, bridle	
Cepheus = the branch		Crowned king holding a branch	Alpha Cephei in shoulder	Alderamin = coming quickly as in a circle	Al Derab = coming in a circle
			Beta Cephei in the side	Alfirk = the redeemer	
Andromeda = the set free from death	Sirra = the chained	Woman chained	Alpha Andromedae in head	Alpheratz = the broken down	
			Beta Andromedae in thigh	Mirach = the weak	

8 Aries = ram	Taleh = lamb sent forth	Ram or lamb	Alpha Arietis in head	Hamal = the sheep, gentle	El Nath = wounded
			Beta Arietis in head	Sheratan = bruised	
Cassiopeia = the en-throned, the beautiful		Woman seated on throne hold-ing branch	Alpha Cassiopeiae in breast	Schedar = the freed	Dat al Cursa = the set, the enthroned
			Beta Cassiopeiae	Caph = the branch	
Perseus = the breaker		Armed man holding head of serpents	Alpha Persei in shoulder	Algenib = who carries away	
			Beta Persei in carried head	Algol = evil spirit	Rosh ha Satan = Satan's head
9 Taurus = bull	Shur = bull, coming, ruling	Bull	Alpha Tauri in the eye	Aldebaran = leader, governor	
			Beta Tauri at end of horn (and in foot of Auriga)	El Nath = wounded, slain	
Orion = coming forth as light	Ha-ga-t = this is he who triumphs	Man with belt, sword, carrying lion's head	Alpha Orionis in shoulder	Betelgeuse = coming of the branch	
			Beta Orionis in foot	Rigel = foot, who treads underfoot	
Eridanus = river of the judge		River, fiery river	Alpha Eridani at end	Achernar = after part of river	
			Beta Eridani at other end	Cursa = bent down	
Auriga = shepherd		Man holding goat, two kids	Alpha Aurigae in goat	Capella = female goat	
			Beta Aurigae in arm	Menkalinan = band, chain of goats	

10 Gemini = twins	Thaumim, Pi Mahi = the united	Two human figures	Alpha Geminorum in head	Castor = haste	Apollo = ruler, judge
			Beta Geminorum in other head	Pollux = ruler, judge	Hercules = coming to suffer
Lepus = hare	Arnebo = enemy of him that comes	Hare	Alpha Leporis in shoulder	Arneb = enemy of him that comes	
Canis Major = great dog		Dog	Alpha Canis Majoris	Sirius = the prince	
			Beta Canis Majoris	Mirzam = prince, ruler	
Canis Minor = lesser dog		Dog	Alpha Canis Minoris	Procyon = the redeemer	
			Beta Canis Minoris	Gomeisa = the burdened, bearing for others	
11 Cancer = crab (cer = encircling)	Sartan = who holds. Klaria = cattle-folds	Crab, possibly scarabaeus beetle	Alpha Cancri	Acubens = sheltering, hiding place	
			M 44, star cluster	Praesepe = multitude, offspring	
Ursa Minor = lesser bear		Bear. Livestock enclosure	Beta Ursae Minoris	Kochab = waiting on him who comes	
			Gamma Ursae Minoris	Pherkad = calves, young	(Heb) = redeemed assembly
Ursa Major = great bear	Ash = the assembled	Bear. Livestock enclosure	Alpha Ursae Majoris	Dubhe = herd of animals	(Chaldean) = wealth. (Heb) = strength
			Beta Ursae Majoris	Merak = the flock	(Arab) = purchased

Argo = company of travelers	Now Puppis = stern, Pyxis = compass, Carina = keep, Vela = sail	Ship	Alpha Carinae	Canopus = possession of him who comes	
12 Leo = lion	(Heb, Arab, Syr) = rending lion	Lion	Alpha Leonis in upper foreleg	Regulus = treading underfoot	
			Beta Leonis in tail	Denebola = judge, lord who comes quickly	
Hydra = he is abhorred		Water serpent	Alpha Hydrae at heart	Alphard = the separated	Minchir al Sugia = piercing of the deceiver
Crater = bowl, cup	Al Ches = cup	Cup of God's wrath placed on Hydra's back			
Corvus = crow, raven	Minchir al Gorab = raven piercing	Raven on Hydra	Alpha Corvi in head	Chiba = the accursed	

Appendix B

Taurus

WE MUST resolve an apparent contradiction in Taurus. On the planisphere in Chapter 1, he is a threatening figure, wounding the foot of Auriga and tamed by Perseus. However, in the Story of the Stars (Chapter 6) he is the Deliverer coming to rule. Does Taurus portray evil or does he portray good?

God the Creator has two outstanding characteristics: his holiness and his love. God's holiness means that he hates evil and punishes evildoers. It means terror to those who break his law. We see this in both the Old and New Testaments.

Psalm 7:11 says God is angry every day. A few examples may be seen in Deuteronomy 1:37, 1 Kings 11:9 and 2 Kings 17:18. Jesus showed anger against religious leaders who hindered the truth. See Mark 3:1-6 and John 2:13–16.

Romans 1:18–20 tells us the reason for God's anger: He has revealed himself since the beginning, and we have deliberately turned away.

But God is also love. His love is the theme of the story in the stars. God sent Jesus to bear the penalty of our sin. Isaiah 53 makes clear that Messiah's sufferings were God's will and plan. Although Messiah suffered at the hands of wicked men, it was God's immense love for us behind the bruising of Messiah's heel.

Taurus, then, portrays both God's holy hatred of sin and his great love. Just as Taurus pierces Auriga's foot, God's wrath pierced Messiah on our behalf. Perseus' foot on Taurus' neck depicts Messiah containing God's judgment.

Bibliography

Allen, Richard Hinckley. *Star Names: Their Lore and Meaning*. New York, NY: Dover Publications, Inc., 1963.

Bhanukitsiri, Ron. "TV-102 performed open-heart surgery on Lion." Observing Reports. The Astronomy Connection. http://observers.org/reports/2002.02.22.html (accessed July 13, 2007.)

Bowden, Hugh. *Ancient Civilizations*. New York: Barnes & Noble Books, 2002.

Bullinger, E. W. *The Witness of the Stars*. Grand Rapids, MI: Kregel Publications, 1967.

Book of Jasher. Salt Lake City: J. H. Parry & Company, 1887. http://www.sacred-texts.com/chr/apo/jasher/.

Chittick, Donald E. *The Puzzle of Ancient Man*. Tualatin, OR: Creation Compass, 1997.

Cooper, Bill. *After the Flood*. Chichester, West Sussex: New Wine Press, 1995.

Hislop, Alexander. *The Two Babylons*. London: A. & C. Black, Ltd., 1932.

Keller, Werner. *The Bible As History*. 2d ed. Toronto: Bantam Books, 1982.

Levy, David H. *Skywatching*. The Nature Company Guides. Time-Life Books, 1994.

McBeath, Alastair. "SPAMS Visual Meteor Shower List." Meteor Section. The Society for Popular Astronomy. http://www.popastro.com/sections/meteor/showers.htm (accessed September 12, 2007.)

Morris, Henry. *The Long War Against God*. Grand Rapids, MI: Baker Book House, 1989.

Ridpath, Ian. *The Night Sky: A Guide to the Stars*. Philadelphia, PA: Running Press, 1994.

Rolleston, Frances. *Mazzaroth*. York Beach, ME: Weiser Books, Inc., 2001.

———. Frances Rolleston to Cary Dent, June 17, 1853. In *Letters of Miss Frances Rolleston*, edited by Caroline Dent. London: Rivingtons, 1867.

Ryken, Leland, James C. Wilhoit, Tremper Longman III, Gen. Ed. *Dictionary of Biblical Imagery*, Downers Grove, IL: InterVarsity Press 1998.

Seiss, Joseph. *The Gospel in the Stars*. Grand Rapids, MI: Kregel, 1972.

Unger, Merrill F. *The New Unger's Bible Dictionary*. Chicago, IL: Moody Press, 1988.

Ussher, James. *The Annals of the World*. Revised and updated by Larry and Miriam Pierce. Green Forest, AZ: Master Books, 2003.